WHAT'S UNDER THE GROUND?

ANITA GANERI

SIMON & SCHUSTER
YOUNG BOOKS

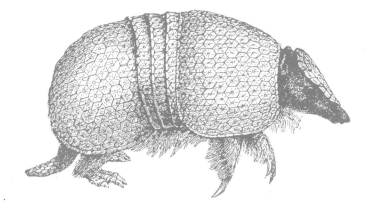

First published in 1993 by
Simon & Schuster Young Books

© 1993 Simon & Schuster Young Books

Simon & Schuster Young Books
Campus 400
Maylands Avenue
Hemel Hempstead
Herts
HP2 7EZ

Design: Jane Hannath

Illustrator: Steven Johnson

Commissioning editor: Debbie Fox

Editor: Jayne Booth

Picture research: Val Mulcahy

Photograph acknowledgements
Front cover: top (t) Ardea (John Mason); centre (c): GeoScience Features Picture Library; bottom (b) and
back cover: Tony Stone Worldwide; Spine: © 1992 Comnstok Inc/Julian Nieman/Susan Griggs. Inside:
Heather Angel, page 14 c; Ardea, page 9 b (John Mason); Biofotos, pages 26 l (Bryn Campbell), 26 r (Soames
Summerhays); British Petroleum, page 32 b; John Cleare/Mountain Camera, pages 38 t, 39 br; Bruce
Coleman, pages 9 t (Charlie Ott), 10 r (M.P.L. Fogden), 13 tl (Jane Burton), 15 l, 16/17 (Patrick Clement),
17 r (Frieder Sauer), 19 c (M.P.L. Fogden), 21 c (G. Ziesler), 24 b (Charlie Ott), 35 tl (Franciso Futil), 35 c
(Keith Gunnar); © 1992 Comnstok Inc/Julian Nieman/Susan Griggs, contents page, 8/9 b; Eastern Electricity,
page 41 r (Eastern Electricity emphasize that safety equipment would now be worn under the Health and
Safety at Work Act); Mary Evans Picture Library, page 39 t; Eye Ubiquitous/TRIP, pages 8 l (N. Wiseman), 38 b
(N. Wiseman); GeoScience Features Picture Library, pages 13 c, 14 b, 23 br, 25 c, 31 tr, 31 cr; Robert Harding
Picture Library, pages 8/9, 12, 16 bl, 23 tl; The Image Bank, pages 19 t (Paul McCormick), 22 (Lisl Dennis),
30 l (Michael Rosenfield), 33 l (Eric Meola); Frank Lane Picture Agency, pages 18 t, 18/19, 28 b (E. & D.
Hosking); Magnum, pages 24 t (Michael Nichols), 27 b (Alex Webb), 36 l (Erich Lessing); Mercedes-Benz
(United Kingdom) Ltd, page 31 cl; NHPA, page 20 br (Karl Switak); The Natural History Museum, London,
pages 8 r, 9 c, 29 c, 34 b, 35 b; Oxford Scientific Films, pages 13 tr (Mantis Wildlife Films), 14 t (David
Thompson), 17 l (John Cooke), 18 c (Terry Heathcote), 18 b (Robin Redfern), 19 b (Rodger Jackman), 20 t
(Jack Dermid), 20 bl (Stan Osolinski), 21 b (Jim Frazier); Picturepoint, pages 11 r, 13 b, 23 tr, 23 c, 23 bl,
25 b, 27 t, 27 c, 28 t, 29t, 29 b, 31 tl, 33 r, 36 r, 37 t, 37 cr, 39 bl, 41 l; Planet Earth Pictures, pages 10 l (David
George), 15 r (Hans C. Heap), 16 t (Steve Hopkin); Science Photo Library, pages 11 l (Adam Hart-Davis), 32 t
(Hattie Young), 34 t and 35 tr (John Reader), 40 b (Will & Deni McIntyre); The Shrine of The Book, Israel
Museum, Jerusalem, page 37 cl; Sotheby's, page 31 b; Tony Stone Worldwide, page 37 b; Survival Anglia,
page 21 t (Alan Root); Thames Water Utilities, page 40 t, 40 c; Zefa, pages 25 t, 30 r.

The author and publishers would like to
thank Mrs Pat Graham and the Ove Arup
Partnership for their assistance.

Typeset by: Goodfellow and Egan, Cambridge

Printed and bound: in Hong Kong by Wing King Tong

A CIP catalogue record for this book is available from the British Library

ISBN 0 7500 1231 5

CONTENTS

Introduction

YOU ONLY HAVE TO LOOK around you to see how varied the landscape is above ground. But what about the hidden world beneath your feet? A journey to the centre of the Earth would take you first through solid, rocky ground. This is called the crust. It is broken into huge pieces, called plates. These drift, very slowly, on the layer below. This layer is called the mantle. It is made of very hot, molten (liquid) rock. The next layer down is the outer core. It is made of molten metals, such as nickel and iron. The inner core at the centre of the Earth is a solid ball of metal, held together by enormous pressure. The temperature here is about 4,500°C. This book looks at the amazing hidden world under the ground.

There are chapters on living things, natural features, natural resources, archaeology and transport and communication.

NATURAL RESOURCES

The ground provides us with many valuable products. Building stone comes from rocks in the Earth's crust, together with metals, precious gems and other minerals. We also rely on the Earth's supply of oil, gas and coal to heat and light our homes, schools and offices.

TRANSPORT AND COMMUNICATION

Many people travel underground every day, on underground railways and through tunnels. These have been dug under towns and cities, through mountainsides and under the sea bed. Tunnels also carry water and sewage pipes, and electricity and telephone cables. Putting all these services under the ground prevents the surface getting too crowded and keeps them out of sight.

NATURAL FEATURES

In some places, the ground under your feet is riddled with natural caves and tunnels carved out of the rock by rainwater. Delicate stalactites and stalagmites decorate many of the caves. Natural features, such as volcanoes and geysers, are also formed as a result of activity underground. Earthquakes cause the ground to shake as the crustal plates move.

ARCHAEOLOGY

Our knowledge of the prehistoric past comes solely from the fossil records in the Earth's crust. Without these, we would never have known about the dinosaurs or about our earliest human ancestors. The rediscovery of long-lost cities and treasures has also added to our knowledge about the peoples of the past. Some of the first dinosaur fossils ever found were of an iguanodon (right). It lived about 125–110 million years ago.

LIVING THINGS

Hundreds of thousands of plants and animals live in the soil which covers the ground. Plants put down their roots for anchorage and to absorb water and minerals. Some animals, such as moles and earthworms, spend most of their lives underground and have special adaptations to help them navigate and find food. Other animals shelter in burrows, but emerge to hunt for their food.

Plants underground

UNLESS A TREE has been uprooted in a storm, or you have been weeding in the garden, you usually only see the parts of a plant showing above ground. But there is plant activity underground too. A plant's roots grow down into the soil, pulled by the force of gravity. They also branch out to the sides in order to anchor the plant more firmly in the ground. The roots take up water and minerals from the soil. These are carried up the plant to its leaves where they are used to make food. Green plants can make their own food in a process called photosynthesis. Many of the plants on these two pages have roots specially adapted to suit a particular environment.

CREOSOTE BUSHES

Creosote bushes grow in the desert where water is hard to find. Instead of wasting energy searching for water deep down, a creosote bush uses its huge mesh of rootlets to take in tiny particles of water which form around rocks just under the surface.

MANGROVES

Mangroves live in muddy, tropical estuaries where rivers meet the sea. They grow a mass of 'stilt' roots from their trunks to anchor them in the mud as the tides wash in and out. There is very little oxygen in the muddy water. So some of the roots poke up out of the water to get oxygen so the trees can breathe.

TREE ROOTS

Each year, a tree's roots grow longer and more branching. This allows them to collect water from a larger area and to support the growing tree. The roots grow longer at their tips, where the cells divide. The root cap protects the delicate tip as it pushes through the soil. Tiny growths, called root hairs, absorb water and minerals from the ground.

Inside a root

Root hairs

Root cap *Root tip*

HOW SEEDS GROW

A seed contains a new plant and a store of food. If it lands in a suitable place, it grows a first root (a radicle) and a first shoot (a plumule). This growth is called germination. The plant uses the food store until its leaves are developed enough for photosynthesis.

BANYAN TREES

Banyan trees grow in parts of Asia where heavy monsoon rains often flood the ground. The trees grow special roots for extra anchorage in the mud. These roots hang down from the banyan's branches. They take root in the soil and grow into thick pillars. One banyan tree in India has over 300 of these supporting pillars.

Roots

APART FROM PROVIDING anchorage in the soil and taking in water and minerals, some plant roots are modified to store food. These food stores help plants to survive over winter when the ground is cold or frozen and does not contain enough water for the plants to make food and grow. The plants shoot up again in the warmer weather of spring. These roots include carrots, radishes and parsnips. They not only provide food for new plants but for animals and human beings too. Other underground plant parts, such as bulbs, corms and tubers, also act as food stores. They are not roots, but modified stems and leaves.

BULBS

Some plants, including hyacinths, daffodils, onions and garlic, form bulbs in order to survive the winter. A bulb is a short stem surrounded by thick, fleshy leaves which contain stores of sugary food. The bulb spends the winter underground. In spring, it produces a new plant which uses the stored food to grow. As it grows, the plant sends some of the food it makes to the bases of its leaves. When the leaves die, their bases swell and form a new bulb.

CORMS

Corms are similar to bulbs but they store food in their short, swollen underground stems, not in their leaves. Crocuses and anemones are among the types of plants which form corms.

TAP ROOTS

Carrots, radishes and parsnips are swollen tap roots. These are the first, and biggest, of the plants' roots. In the wild, most carrots have straggly white roots. The only type with orange roots grows in Afghanistan. It is thought that the carrots we eat were cultivated from this variety.

AERIAL ROOTS

Some plants do not have roots, or any underground parts. Some tropical orchids grow high up on tree branches. Their roots hang in the air, absorbing all the water they need in the form of water vapour. Other plants, such as ivy, use aerial roots for climbing.

TUBERS

Tubers are short, swollen underground stems which contain stores of starchy food. In the spring, buds sprout from the tuber and grow into new plants. As its food store is used up, the tuber shrinks and shrivels. Potatoes and yams are types of tuber.

RHIZOMES

Rhizomes are thick stems which grow horizontally under the ground. They do not store food, like carrots, but allow plants to grow and spread very quickly. Roots and shoots grow along the rhizome. These develop into new plants and the section of rhizome connecting them dies. Irises and ferns grow from rhizomes.

DID YOU KNOW

People living on Kyushu Island, Japan, grow record-breaking radishes. The huge radishes are cultivated in the rich lava soil which surrounds Mount Sakhurajima, an active volcano on the island.

Life in the Soil

I N MANY PLACES, the ground is covered in a layer of soil. The layer may be just a few centimetres thick or several metres thick. Soil is made up of tiny chips of rock, sand and clay, air, water and the rotting remains of plants and animals. The latter form a jelly-like substance called humus, which makes the soil rich and fertile. Soil is vitally important. Without it, plants would have nowhere to grow and animals and human beings would have nothing to eat. The soil is also home to millions of creatures, large and small. In fact, more animals live in the soil than in any other habitat on Earth.

AMAZING BUT TRUE

A teaspoonful of soil contains over 10 billion bacteria. They feed on dead and decaying plants and animals helping to convert them into humus. In doing this, they recycle minerals which plants need to grow. They also help to bind the particles of soil together.

EARTHWORMS

Earthworms are an important part of the soil community. As the worms tunnel, they eat some of the soil. It passes through their bodies and is discarded as worm casts on the surface. This helps to mix the various parts of the soil together. The worms' tunnels also act as air and drainage passages to keep the soil healthy.

FUNGI

Fungi are made of masses of tiny tube-like threads, called hyphae. Some of the hyphae form a 'fruiting body' above ground, but most of the fungus is underground. The hyphae feed off living or dead matter in the soil, digesting it with special juices, then absorbing it.

Fly agaric

Fruiting body

Hyphae

TERMITE MOUNDS

Termites are tiny, blind creatures about the size of grains of rice. Yet they build huge towers over 6 metres high out of mud and saliva. This mixture forms a type of cement which sets rock hard. Some termites also build vast underground cellars and passageways about 2 metres below the surface. These provide shelter and keep the rest of the nest cool. The colony of termites living in the nest may number 10 million or more.

DIGGER WASPS

As their name suggests, digger wasps dig their nests in the ground or in dead wood. The female digs the nest, then catches an insect, such as a fly. She paralyses it with her sting. Then she drags it to the nest and lays an egg on it. When the wasp grub hatches, the fly provides it with its first, ready-made meal.

SOIL PROFILE

Soil forms in layers. The dark topsoil is full of rich humus. In the layer below it, called the subsoil, the humus is mixed with tiny stones and sand. It is lighter in colour than the topsoil and far less fertile. The lower layers contain larger stones broken off the rocks below.

MINING BEES

Mining bees dig their nest burrows in the ground, often in garden lawns. The females stock the nests with honey and lay their eggs in them. Then they seal the nest up and abandon it. The newly hatched bee grubs feed off the stores of honey until they are old enough to fend for themselves.

Minibeasts

MANY SMALL ANIMALS LIVE in the soil, among the plant roots and under the leaf litter for shelter and safety. Out in the open, they are unprotected against predators such as birds. These 'minibeasts' all have special features to help them find their food, their way about and a safe place to hide. Among the huge variety of mini-beasts found in the soil are spiders, beetles, centipedes and woodlice.

WOODLICE

Woodlice live under stones and among the rotting leaf litter around trees. They come out at night to feed on decaying plants. They curl into a tight ball if danger threatens. Woodlice are crustaceans, related to shrimps and crabs.

Violet ground beetle

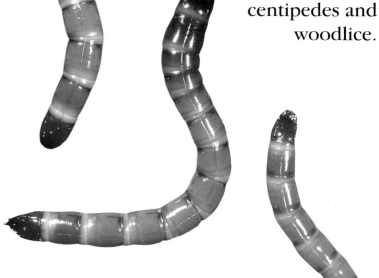

GROUND BEETLES

Like woodlice, ground beetles are nocturnal creatures. During the day they rest in dark, damp crannies under stones or logs. These beetles have big, powerful jaws for catching their prey of slugs. Ground beetle larvae (young) are also fierce predators.

Adult click beetle

WIREWORMS

Wireworms are the tough-bodied, shiny larvae of click beetles. They live and feed underground on plant roots. They are often found on farmland where they cause a great deal of damage by eating away at the roots of potatoes and cereal crops. Adult click beetles are nocturnal. They hide among plant roots during the day.

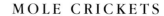

MOLE CRICKETS

These unusual insects have short, spade-like front legs for digging through the soil. They can fly but spend most of their time underground where they feed on insect larvae and roots. The male's burrow acts like a loudspeaker. It amplifies his courtship song so that it can be heard up to 2 kilometres away.

GALL WASPS

Female gall wasps lay their eggs in the roots and leaves of oak trees. The area around the eggs swells up to form a gall. The larvae hatch and feed inside the gall until they are ready to emerge as adults.

ANTLION AMBUSH

Antlion larvae have an ingenious way of ambushing and trapping their prey of ants and other small insects. They dig funnel-shaped pits in the sand and lie in wait at the bottom with their large jaws pointing upwards. Ants slide down the sides of the traps and are quickly snapped up.

TRAPDOOR SPIDERS

A female trapdoor spider (above) digs her burrow in the ground and lines it with silk. Then she makes a circular door out of more silk and soil and fixes it to the burrow with a silk hinge. During the day, the door is tightly shut. At night, however, the spider opens the door and pokes out her four front legs. Any passing insect is quickly grabbed and dragged into the burrow.

Burrowers

THE TYPE OF HOME an animal has depends on how much protection it needs from predators, how much shelter it needs from the weather and the sort of building materials available. Underground burrows are one of the most widespread and versatile types of animal home. They may be dug in the soil, or in sand or even in snow. Some animals spend most of their lives underground; others shelter and rest in their burrows during the day but come out at night to find food. Other animals only use burrows as safe places to have and raise their young.

MOLES

Moles are superbly adapted for underground living. They have strong, spade-like front feet for digging. They have very poor eyesight but find their food of earthworms by smell. They also use the sensitive whiskers on their faces for feeling their way around.

KINGFISHERS

In the breeding season, kingfishers dig out tunnels in the river bank and build their nests at the far end. The tunnels may be a metre long. The female lays six to eight eggs. Many birds' eggs have coloured shells for camouflage. Kingfisher eggs are white. They are so well hidden inside the burrow that they have no need of camouflage.

MOLEHILLS

Molehills are the only evidence you may ever see of a mole. Moles can dig tunnels over 100 metres long. From time to time, they push the earth they excavate to the surface. An extra-large molehill is formed over their main nest chamber.

PUFFINS

Puffins often gather in their thousands to breed. They nest in cliff-top burrows. They may dig these themselves, using their sharp claws. Quite often, though, they use abandoned rabbit holes as ready-made nests. The female lays a single egg deep inside the burrow.

MARMOTS

In winter, marmots hibernate in deep, hay-lined burrows to avoid the cold. A whole family of up to 15 animals huddles together in one burrow for warmth. The marmots may hibernate for over six months. During this time their metabolism slows down and their body temperature and breathing rate drop drastically.

BADGER SETTS

Badgers dig their setts among tree roots or in woodland banks, up to 2 metres underground. Each sett is a maze of tunnels, chambers and air holes, entrances and exits. The bed chambers are lined with straw and bracken which is taken outside and aired on warm days. The same sett may be used by several generations of badgers for as long as 200 years.

GERBILS

In their desert home, gerbils shelter from the scorching daytime sun in underground burrows. Just 10 centimetres down, the temperature may be 17°C lower than above ground. The gerbils plug the burrow entrance to stop any precious moisture escaping. They come out to feed in the coolness of the night.

AMAZING BUT TRUE

Blind snakes are small, burrowing snakes. One type, called the flowerpot snake, spread from Asia to Europe hidden inside earth-filled flowerpots. The snakes quickly became widespread because the females can breed on their own. There are no male flowerpot snakes.

Unusual animals underground

SOME VERY UNUSUAL animals live underground, including fish. Some never come to the surface at all; others only venture outside to feed or get water. Like the minibeasts and burrowers, however, they are all adapted in some way to their subterranean lifestyles.

CAVE SALAMANDERS

Cave salamanders live in the dim light near the entrances to caves. The damp atmosphere of the cave suits these creatures perfectly. They need to keep their skin moist so they can breathe through it.

BURROWING OWLS

Burrowing owls live on the American prairies. There are very few trees on the prairies to offer shelter so the owls lay their eggs in underground burrows. These are usually old prairie dog burrows which the owls enlarge with their strong claws. The parents spend the day hunting for insects to feed to their chicks.

PUPFISH

The devil's hole pupfish is only found in one place in the world. This is a tiny, water-filled hole about 18 metres under the Nevada Desert in the USA. The pupfish holds the title of the world's most restricted fish.

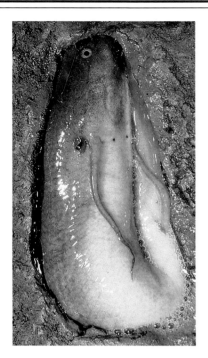

LUNGFISH

African lungfish live in swamps and pools which often dry up in the hot season. Then the lungfish seal themselves into burrows in the soft mud and live off their own muscle tissue until the rains come again. They can survive like this for up to three years. They have simple lungs, as well as gills, for breathing on land.

CAVE SWIFTLETS

Huge colonies of swiftlets live in enormous caves in Asia. Some build their nests out of their own saliva and stick them onto the cave walls. People risk their lives to collect these nests which are sold to make bird's nest soup.

HAIRY ARMADILLO

Armadillos can dig with lightning speed to escape from enemies. They also excavate large burrow systems, pushing the soil aside with their strong front feet and their noses. They hold their breath to avoid taking in too much dust.

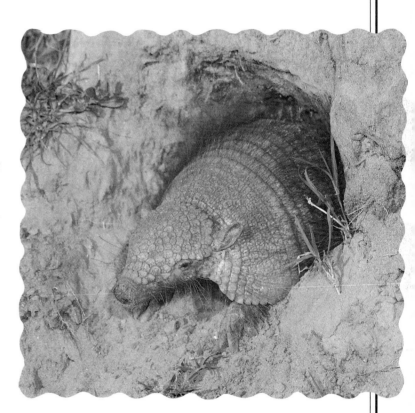

DID YOU KNOW

Each year a staggering 20 million female Mexican free-tailed bats gather in Bracken Cave, Texas, USA. They use the cave to have their young. They collect here after their migration from Mexico.

WATER-HOLDING FROG

The water-holding frog lives in the Australian desert. When there is a rare fall of rain, it comes out of its underground burrow and absorbs water through its skin. This makes the frog swell up like a small balloon. Then it retreats back underground with its own private water supply.

Caves and potholes

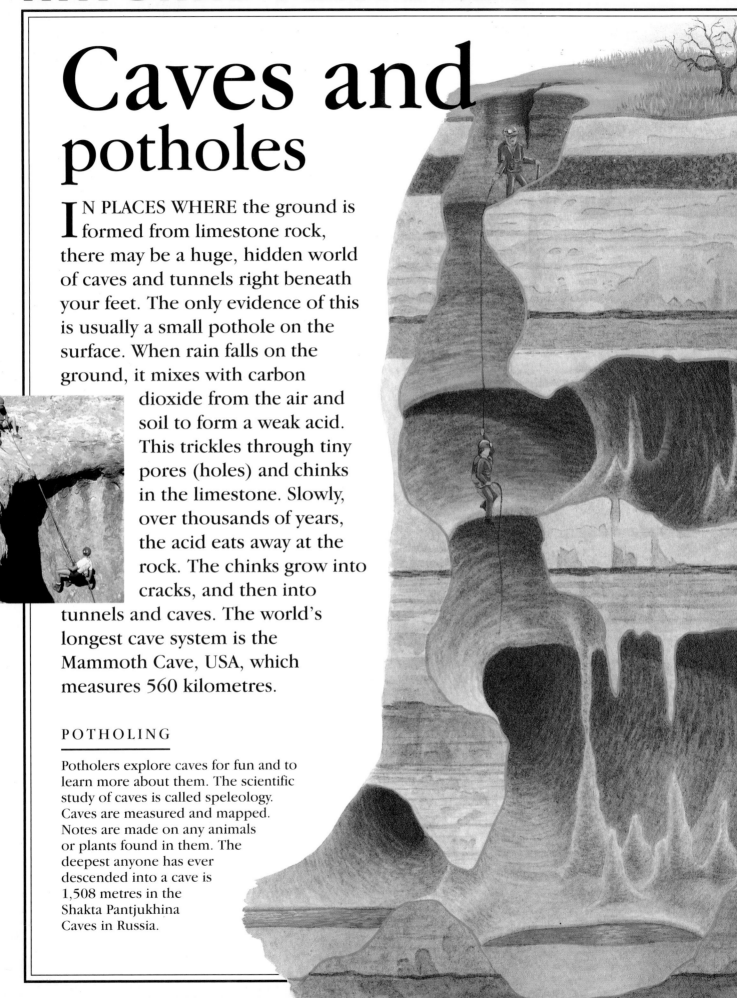

IN PLACES WHERE the ground is formed from limestone rock, there may be a huge, hidden world of caves and tunnels right beneath your feet. The only evidence of this is usually a small pothole on the surface. When rain falls on the ground, it mixes with carbon dioxide from the air and soil to form a weak acid. This trickles through tiny pores (holes) and chinks in the limestone. Slowly, over thousands of years, the acid eats away at the rock. The chinks grow into cracks, and then into tunnels and caves. The world's longest cave system is the Mammoth Cave, USA, which measures 560 kilometres.

POTHOLING

Potholers explore caves for fun and to learn more about them. The scientific study of caves is called speleology. Caves are measured and mapped. Notes are made on any animals or plants found in them. The deepest anyone has ever descended into a cave is 1,508 metres in the Shakta Pantjukhina Caves in Russia.

ICE CAVES

Caves are sometimes found deep inside glaciers, icebergs and ice sheets. Ice caves inside glaciers are formed when crevasses in the ice do not close completely or when melted water runs underneath the glaciers and carves away the ice. The caves on the right are on Ross Island in Antarctica.

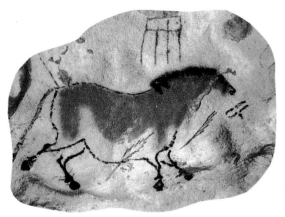

CAVE PAINTING

Prehistoric people left records on the walls of the caves they lived in, in the form of paintings. One of the best of these art galleries is in the Lascaux Caves in France. The 596 paintings of bulls, horses, bison and mammoths are thought to date from the last Ice Age, over 20,000 years ago.

AJANTA

Between 200BC and AD700, Buddhist monks carved out 29 cave temples in the cliff face at Ajanta, India. They had no powerful tools or scaffolding to help them. They began at the top of the cliff and worked their way down through the sandstone, carving out the walls.

CAVE DWELLINGS

In the Cappadocia region of Turkey, there are some extraordinary cone-shaped mounds of volcanic rock. These have been worn into shape over thousands of years. Since the 4th century AD, people have carved out homes and churches inside the cones. In the same region, there are also vast, maze-like underground towns which may be almost 2,000 years old. One town, Derinkuya, was at least eight storeys deep and had room for 15,000 people. To keep intruders out, the entrance passages were blocked off with huge, round stones.

Stalactites and

AS WATER TRICKLES through limestone, it dissolves calcium carbonate (lime) from the rock. Drips of water falling from the roof of a cave leave a ring-shaped deposit of calcium carbonate behind. The rings build up in layers, over hundreds of years, to form a stalactite. Where drips hit the floor, the water may evaporate. The rings of calcium carbonate build upwards to form stalagmites. These stone icicles grow very slowly, at a rate of 1–2 millimetres a year. There is an easy way to remember which is which. Stalactites grow from the ceiling to the ground. Stalagmites grow from the ground to the ceiling.

FABULOUS FORMATIONS

Stalactites and stalagmites which contain pure calcium carbonate are white or clear. But they are often coloured by other minerals dissolved in the water. Stalactites and stalagmites sometimes join to form columns or pillars.

DID YOU KNOW

The longest stalactite known measures 59 metres. It hangs from the roof of the Cueva de Nerja in Spain. The tallest stalagmite is 32 metres high. It was found in a cave in Czechoslovakia.

BALCONY STALACTITES

Balcony stalactites grow downwards from the wall of the cave, not from the ceiling. They are formed by water trickling down the wall. Other features, called curtain stalactites, form when water is blown sideways.

Stalagmites

Rivers and lakes

I F THE WATER TRICKLING down through the ground reaches a layer of hard rock, it cannot travel any further. In some places, it collects as an underground lake or flows through the lowest tunnels as a river. As on land, the water carves the rocks away, widening the tunnels and caves. Less than 1 per cent of all the water in the world lies underground. The largest underground lake is in the Drachenhauchloch Cave in Namibia in Africa. The lake lies 60 metres under the ground. Its water is 90 metres deep.

THE BLUE GROTTO

The Blue Grotto shown at the top *(Grotto Azzura)* is found on the island of Capri in the Bay of Naples, Italy. It can only be reached by boat. As sunlight enters the grotto, it is refracted (bent) by the water. As a result, the water and the grotto walls shimmer with a silvery blue light.

THE CAVES OF DRAC

The Caves of Drac in Majorca are famous for their underground lakes and dramatic limestone formations. Some of these formations are thought to look like dragons. This gives the caves their name – *Drac* means 'dragon' in Spanish. Musicians give concerts from boats on the lakes.

THE RIVER STYX

The ancient Greeks believed that an underground river, the Styx, formed the boundary between the world of the living and the underworld. When people died, their souls crossed the river to reach the underworld. Its entrance was guarded by the three-headed dog, Cerberus.

Volcanoes, geysers and earthquakes

THE ROCKS OF the Earth's crust are constantly, if very slowly, drifting on the molten (liquid) layers below them. The ground may feel firm and stable, but, in fact, it is never still. The plates which make up the crust jostle for position, causing earthquakes on land and sea. The molten rock itself adds to the Earth's restlessness. In some places, it shoots up through the crust as a volcano or heats underground water until it gushes up as a geyser. The key to these movements is the enormous heat stored inside the Earth. It is known as geothermal energy.

MOUNT EREBUS

At the South Pole, the surface of the ground may be covered in ice, but the rocks underneath are just as hot as elsewhere. Mount Erebus (below) stands on Ross Island, Antarctica. It is the world's most southerly active volcano.

VOLCANOES

Volcanoes erupt when molten rock, called magma, deep underground is forced upwards. This happens when there is a build-up of pressure underground. The rock bursts out or seeps up through cracks in the Earth's crust. It is now called lava. If the lava is thick and cools quickly, it forms a cone-shaped volcano. If it is thin and flows some distance before cooling, it forms a flat, shield volcano. Lava can flow at speeds of over 600km/h.

GEYSERS

The word *geysir* means 'gusher' in Icelandic. Geysers occur in places where there are lots of volcanoes, such as Iceland, New Zealand and parts of the USA. Red-hot magma heats underground water until it is under so much pressure that it shoots out of the ground in a scalding fountain. Old Faithful geyser (right) is in Yellowstone National Park, USA. It has erupted every hour or so for the past 100 years.

OLD FAITHFUL GEYSER

HOT MUD SPRINGS

Natural hot water springs are found where heated underground water seeps up to the surface. It does not gush up, however, like a geyser. Sometimes, minerals dissolve in the water on its way up and it bubbles to the surface as mud. The mud may be brown, yellow or red depending on the colour of the minerals in the water.

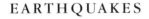

DID YOU KNOW

On 27 August 1883, the volcanic island of Krakatoa erupted with the loudest bang ever. The noise could be heard 4,800 kilometres away. The entire northern half of the island blew apart and collapsed into the sea.

EARTHQUAKES

When two crustal plates try to push past each other then suddenly slip, the ground shakes. This is an earthquake. There are about 500,000 earthquakes a year. Most are too weak to be felt but a few cause terrible damage. Cracks open in the ground and buildings collapse, causing loss of life and homes.

Rocks and minerals

THE HARD GROUND beneath your feet, together with the mountains and the sea bed, are made of rocks which formed millions of years ago. These rocks are made of chemicals, called minerals, which occur naturally inside the Earth. They include carbon, iron, quartz and so on. Minerals are made up of different elements. These are basic chemicals, such as oxygen and silicon. Different types of rocks contain a single mineral or a combination of minerals. There is a great variety of rocks. They have different textures, colours and shapes. But they all belong to one of three families, depending on how they were formed. The families are igneous, sedimentary and metamorphic rocks.

Fatehpur Sikri, near Agra, India

IGNEOUS ROCKS

The Giant's Causeway (above) in Northern Ireland is made of columns of basalt, a type of igneous rock. The word igneous means 'fiery'. These rocks were formed by volcanic eruptions, when lava cooled and hardened. Apart from basalt, the igneous family includes granite, obsidian and pumice.

SEDIMENTARY ROCKS

Sedimentary rocks include limestone and sandstone, sometimes used in building. These rocks formed in layers from grains of other rock and sand. Many were originally part of the sea bed and also contain fossils of shells and tiny sea creatures. Over thousands of years, the weight of the upper layers pressed down on the lower layers and turned them to stone.

METAMORPHIC ROCKS

Metamorphic means 'changed'. Metamorphic rocks form when igneous or sedimentary rocks are pushed back into the Earth. They are melted and changed by the enormous heat and pressure to form different rocks. Metamorphic rocks include marble, slate and gneiss. Marble is a 'changed' form of limestone. In Italy, it is cut from the mountainside for building and making statues.

CRYSTALS

Minerals sometimes form in clusters of regular-shaped crystals inside rocks. Quartz is one of the most common types of mineral. It often forms six-sided, milky-white crystals inside volcanic rocks. People used to think that these crystals were permanently frozen lumps of ice.

MINERAL HARDNESS

Minerals are graded according to how hard they are, on a scale of one to 10. Diamond is the hardest mineral there is, and the hardest substance on Earth. It can only be cut using another diamond. Talc is the softest mineral. It can be scratched with a fingernail.

FLINT TOOLS

Flint is a type of chalcedony, a variety of quartz. It is often found in lumpy nodules, which are white on the outside and black inside. Flint breaks into sharp pieces. This is why prehistoric people found it so useful. They used flint to make tools, such as axe-heads and arrow-heads.

Mining

IN SOME PLACES, coal, metal ores and other resources lie near the surface of the ground. They can simply be scooped up or blasted out with explosives. This type of mining is called open-cast mining. But many metals, gemstones and so on lie deep under the Earth's surface. Geologists first have to study the rocks to see what resources they might contain. Then mines have to be dug through solid rock to get them out. Today, many mines are highly mechanised. In the most modern mines, underground vehicles and machinery are controlled by computer from the surface. Where miners do work underground, special attention is paid to their safety.

COAL MINING

Coal is found both on the surface and deep underground. In early coal mines, miners crawled along narrow, underground tunnels and hacked the coal out with picks and shovels. It was loaded into carts and pulled to the surface by ponies and young children. (There is more about coal on page 33).

SLATE QUARRYING

Slate is a type of blue-grey metamorphic rock formed from mudstone and shale. It is quarried and used as a building material. Slate splits easily into thin sheets or slabs. This quality, called slaty cleavage, has proved useful for making roof and floor tiles, blackboards and for lining snooker tables.

GOLD DIGGING

Many countries keep their national savings in the form of gold bars, called bullion. Gold is so precious because it is so rare and difficult to find. One tonne of rock may have to be mined to collect a piece of gold the size of a sugar lump.

IRON ORE

Rocks containing metals are called ores. Iron is often found in an ore called haematite (below). This is mined, then heated in a huge oven called a blast furnace. The iron inside the ore melts and can then be collected and used. It hardens as it cools. About 900 million tonnes of iron ore are mined worldwide each year.

STEEL

Some iron is melted down and mixed with carbon to make a stronger metal, called steel. This type of mixture is known as an alloy. Steel is used to make cars, tools and machinery. Cutlery is often made from stainless steel. This is steel which has been mixed with the metal chromium, to prevent it going rusty.

GEMSTONES...

The rocks of the Earth's crust contain about 3,000 different types of minerals. About 100 of these are so rare and precious that they are specially classed as gemstones. They include emeralds, such as the one on the left.

... AND JEWELLERY

In their natural state, gemstones are rough and dull. But they are cut and polished to make them sparkle. They can then be used to make beautiful jewellery. This stunning brooch belonged to the Duchess of Windsor. It is studded with exquisite diamonds, rubies, emeralds and sapphires.

Fossil Fuels

OIL, GAS AND COAL are usually found deep underground. They are known as fossil fuels because they formed millions of years ago from the remains of prehistoric plants and animals. Oil and gas are found in rocks which were once part of the sea bed. Some of these rocks are still under the sea, but some are now part of dry land. Oil and gas formed from the bodies of tiny sea creatures which died and sank to the sea bed. They were buried under layers of sand and mud which eventually turned into solid rock, trapping the oil and gas. Fossil fuels provide most of our heat, light and fuel. They are mined and drilled for all over the world. There is more about fossils on pages 34 – 35.

OIL EXTRACTION

Oil companies explore and drill for oil all over the world – in the desert, in the ice caps around the Arctic, in the jungle and, of course, at sea. On land, a machine called a nodding donkey (above) is sometimes used to extract small amounts of oil. A shaft is drilled into the ground and the nodding donkey is used to pump the oil out.

THE DRILL BIT

A rotating drill is often used to cut through the rock to reach the oil or gas below. It consists of long lengths of steel pipe with a drill bit at the end. This has very tough teeth of diamond or tungsten carbide.

DID YOU KNOW
The world's largest oil field is the Ghawar field in the Saudi Arabian desert. It covers an area of 8,400 square kilometres which is almost as big as the Mediterranean island of Cyprus.

AT THE REFINERY

The oil that comes out of the ground is called crude oil. It is a mixture of thick and thin oils, and other chemicals. The oil is transported to a refinery where it is separated into various products, such as petrol, diesel oil and kerosene. The thickest oils are used to make bitumen, a road covering. Other chemicals in the oil are made into plastics, paints, detergents, fertilisers, nylon and other materials.

PIPELINES

Oil wells are often far away from the nearest refineries. The oil has to be carried overland by a long, steel pipeline. In empty, barren areas such as deserts, the pipeline may lie on the surface of the ground. In other places, a trench is dug and the pipe is buried underground. Gas pipelines transport gas to a larger grid system which supplies homes, offices and factories.

AMAZING BUT TRUE

People in China were drilling for oil over 2,000 years ago. They discovered the oil as they were digging for brine (very salty water). They used the brine to provide salt for their cattle. To reach the oil, they dropped a chisel-like tool onto the rock, hundreds and hundreds of times. It took years to drill a well.

COAL SWAMPS

Coal began to form about 300 million years ago in the Carboniferous ('coal-bearing') age. Huge plants which grew around swamps died and were covered and squashed by layers of mud and more plants. This squeezed the water out of them and they turned from peat into coal.

Fossil Hunting

THE ROCKS OF THE EARTH'S crust not only provide us with metals, minerals, oil and gas. They are also our only source of information about life in prehistoric times. These records are in the form of fossils. Fossils formed millions of years ago. When a plant or animal died, the soft parts of its body rotted away. The hard parts, such as teeth, shells and bones were buried under mud and sand. Their cells were replaced by minerals and they gradually turned to stone. Fossil-bearing rocks were usually buried deep underground. In places, erosion and movements of the crust have brought them to the surface. Scientists are able to excavate them and piece them together. The chances of something forming a fossil were extremely small so any finds are very exciting.

PILTDOWN MAN

In 1912, a human skull was found in Britain. Scientists thought it was about a million years old. But, 40 years later, the skull was proved to be a fake. It was, in fact, part of an orang-utan skull. The million-year-old teeth had been glued on!

IGUANODON

The first iguanodon fossils were found in 1822 by an English doctor, Gideon Mantell. He found some teeth, then the rest of the dinosaur in a quarry. The iguanodon lived about 125–110 million years ago. It grew up to 9 metres long. It had a large, spiked thumb which it probably used to defend itself from enemies.

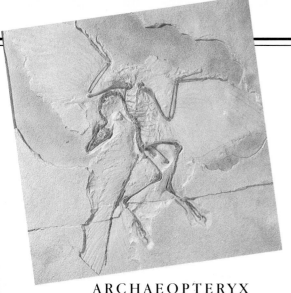

ARCHAEOPTERYX

In 1861, an amazing fossil was found in Solnhofen, Germany. It showed a bird-like animal, its body covered in feathers. This was the first evidence of feathers ever found. Scientists named the bird archaeopteryx, which means 'ancient feather'. It was about the size of a pigeon and lived some 150 million years ago.

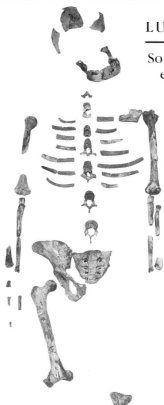

LUCY

So far, the fossils of our earliest ancestors have only been found in Africa. The most complete fossil is that of a female which the excavators nicknamed 'Lucy'. She died about three million years ago, aged about 40.

AMAZING BUT TRUE

Dinosaurs lived from about 220–65 million years ago. But no one knew they had ever existed until about 150 years ago. A fossil bone was described as early as 1677. But scientists thought it belonged to a giant man. It was later found to be a thigh bone of the huge dinosaur, megalosaurus.

DIGGING DEEP

Digging up fossils is a long, painstaking job. First, the rock is chiselled and chipped away. Then photographs are taken of the site. The fossils are wrapped in plaster of Paris to protect them as they are finally, very gently, dug out of the rock. Then they are numbered, labelled and taken to a laboratory to be analysed and carefully pieced together.

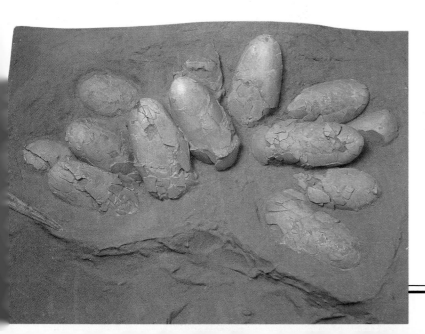

EGGS AND NESTS

Dinosaur babies hatched out of eggs, just like many of their reptile relations today. The parents laid the eggs in nests, hollowed out of the sand or soil. Our first evidence of this came from the Gobi Desert in Mongolia. In 1923, scientists found several nests and over 50 fossil eggs belonging to a group of protoceratops. The eggs were laid about 90 million years ago.

Hidden Treasures

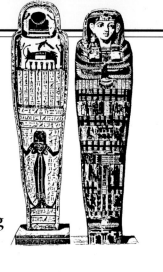

ARCHAEOLOGISTS SOMETIMES make thrilling discoveries of ancient treasures, and even long-lost towns and cities, which have lain buried and forgotten under the ground for centuries. Some are found quite by accident as scientists or builders are looking for something else. Others involve months or years of detective work on the part of the archaeologists. They may use historical accounts, written records and other artefacts to track down a site. Then they begin to excavate in the hope that they are right. These discoveries provide us with fascinating and valuable information about how and where people lived in the past.

KNOSSOS

The palace of Knossos, on the Greek island of Crete, was the centre of Minoan civilisation. People were already living there over 5,000 years ago. The palace was destroyed by fire in about 1375BC. Its remains were rediscovered in 1894 by the English archaeologist, Sir Arthur Evans.

KING TUTANKHAMUN

Tutankhamun was an Egyptian king who died in about 1352BC. For many years, archaeologists had searched for his tomb in the Valley of the Kings. Then, in 1922, Howard Carter made the breakthrough. He dug his way into Tutankhamun's tomb and became the first person in over 3,000 years to see the dead king's hoard of priceless treasures. They included the gold death mask, shown on the left.

DEAD SEA SCROLLS

The Dead Sea Scrolls were found, quite by chance, in about 1947 in caves above the Dead Sea in Israel. The Scrolls were written between the 2nd century BC and the 2nd century AD. The text is mostly from the Old Testament of the Bible, written in the Hebrew, Aramaic and Greek languages. The Scrolls are made from strips of sheepskin. They had been hidden inside clay jars.

POMPEII

The Roman town of Pompeii was buried under hot ash when Mount Vesuvius erupted in AD79. It was rediscovered in 1748. Many of its buildings and paintings had been well preserved. There were also hollows left by the bodies of people who had tried to flee. These were used to make plaster casts of the victims.

THE TERRACOTTA ARMY

In 1974, villagers near the city of Xi'an in China began to dig a well. Instead of water, they made an amazing discovery about 5 metres underground. They found rows and rows of life-size terracotta soldiers. Some were holding real weapons. There were about 8,000 warriors in this extraordinary army. They had been made over 2,000 years ago to guard the tomb of the Emperor Qin Shi Huang.

Underground Travel

IN MANY BUSY TOWNS and cities all over the world, people travel under the ground every day on their way to school or to work. There are 67 underground railway systems in the world. Without them, the streets above would get even busier and more congested and the cities would grind to a halt. At least you don't get stuck in traffic jams underground! Underground travel is also necessary in very mountainous areas. Where there is no easy way for vehicles to go over or round the mountain, tunnels are drilled through the mountain itself. These have led to a huge reduction in travelling times in places such as the European Alps. Rail tunnels have also been dug under the sea bed to allow passengers and goods to travel quickly and conveniently from place to place.

THROUGH THE EIGER

The rail tunnel above goes straight through the Swiss Alps. The train enters the tunnel in the side of the Eiger at a place called Eigergletscher. It then travels 7.5 kilometres deep inside the mountains before emerging again.

THE MOSCOW UNDERGROUND

The Moscow Metro in Russia is the world's busiest underground railway system. On a normal day, over seven million passengers travel on it. It has about 140 stations and almost 230 kilometres of track. The longest tunnel on the Metro, and the longest subway tunnel in the world, is about 38 kilometres long.

DID YOU KNOW

The world's longest escalator is on the St Petersburg underground. It drops almost 60 metres. The first escalator, designed in 1894, was based on the same principle as a conveyor belt.

THE FIRST UNDERGROUND

The London Underground was the first underground railway in the world. Its first stretch of line opened in January 1863. The first underground trains were steam powered so the tunnels had to be well ventilated. The first electric trains were used in the 1890s. Today, about 500 trains run on the Underground along about 410 kilometres of track. There are over 270 stations.

ROAD TUNNELS

The world's longest road tunnel is the St Gotthard tunnel. It stretches for 16.32 kilometres through the Swiss Alps between Switzerland and Italy. It was opened in 1980. The tunnel on the right was built to replace a road which was often hit by avalanches.

THE SEIKAN RAIL TUNNEL

The Seikan rail tunnel runs under the sea between the islands of Honshu and Hokkaido in Japan. At 53.85 kilometres, it is the longest rail tunnel in the world. The tunnel took 20 years to complete. It was first tried out in 1988.

THE CHANNEL TUNNEL

The Channel Tunnel will run some 70 metres below the sea bed between England and France. Trains will carry passengers, cars and goods. A version of the Channel Tunnel dating from 1802 had people travelling in horse-drawn vehicles.

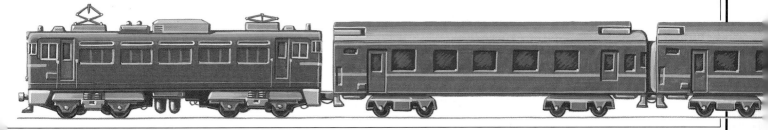

Cables, Homes
and services

APART FROM CARS AND TRAINS, underground tunnels are also used for carrying supplies and services to and from homes, schools, offices and factories. They contain pipes for water, waste and gas, and cables for carrying electricity and phone messages. The different pipes are colour coded to avoid confusion. Drains, grates and man-holes are often the only signs of this tunnel network on the surface. The longest service tunnel of any kind is a water-supply tunnel in New York, USA. It is 168.9 kilometres long. The most important parts of buildings and roads lie hidden underground too. These are the foundations. They support the buildings and stop them sinking into the ground.

WATER PIPES AND SEWERS

Underground pipes carry water to our homes and waste away from them. The pipes are usually made of tough plastic and are laid about a metre underground. This is to prevent any damage from traffic vibration or frost. The waste pipes link into the main sewer system. Some sewers are as big as subway tunnels, although most are about 30 centimetres wide.

TELEPHONE CABLES

Most phone messages travel along underground cables laid in pipes called ducts. A cable is made up of slender glass threads, called optical fibres. Each fibre is no thicker than a human hair yet it can carry thousands of phone calls. Some phone messages travel along overhead wires. But these are easily damaged by storms.

ELECTRICITY

Electricity is produced in power stations. It travels into a network of cables called the national grid. Then it travels through more cables to homes, schools and offices. It reaches each room through sockets in the wall. Some cables are suspended from overhead pylons. Others are buried in deep trenches under the ground. The cables are covered in steel or plastic 'sleeves' for safety.

UNDERGROUND HOMES

Some people have their whole home underground, not just the foundations. Berber people living on the edge of the scorching Sahara Desert in Tunisia live underground to keep cool. Their houses are two to three storeys high and are built around a central courtyard.

FIRM FOUNDATIONS

When a new building is constructed, its foundations are laid first to stop it sinking. Ordinary houses are built on concrete foundations. Tall, heavy skyscrapers need extra-strong foundations. They are supported by concrete or steel rods, called piles, sunk up to 25 metres into the ground.

AMAZING BUT TRUE

A huge system of tunnels and passages 250 kilometres long lies outside the city gates of Rome. They are up to 20 metres underground. These are the catacombs where early Christians buried their dead in the 1st to 5th centuries AD. The catacombs were robbed in the 8th century AD, then forgotten until 1578. There are no bodies in them now.

DEPTH GUIDE

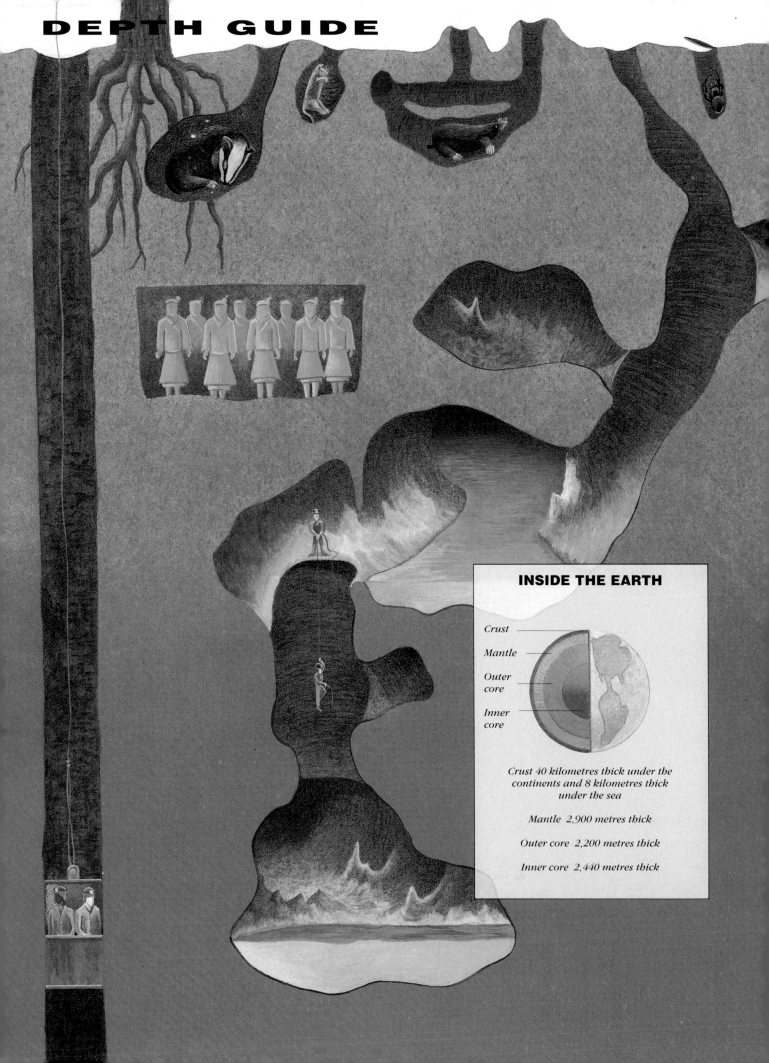

INSIDE THE EARTH

Crust
Mantle
Outer core
Inner core

Crust 40 kilometres thick under the continents and 8 kilometres thick under the sea

Mantle 2,900 metres thick

Outer core 2,200 metres thick

Inner core 2,440 metres thick

INSIDE THE EARTH

Look at the depth guide from left to right and see what's going on beneath your feet. The Earth's crust, the thin outer layer, is 40 kilometres thick, which is ten times the depth of the deepest mine.

- **Deepest mine (3,777 metres)** *Western Deep Levels gold mine, South Africa*
- **Oak tree roots (3 metres deep)**
- **Badger sett (2 metres)**
- **Terracotta Army, China (5 metres)**
- **Largest underground lake (60 metres) (Drachenhauchloch Cave, Namibia)**
- **Gerbil burrows (10 centimetres)**
- **Deepest cave descent (1,508 metres)** *Shakta Pantjukhina Cave, Russia*
- **Mole tunnels (up to 1 metre)**
- **Trapdoor spider burrow (15 centimetres)**
- **Termite nest cellars (2 metres)**
- **Lascaux Cave paintings (6 metres)**
- **Deepest cave (1,602 metres)** *Gouffre Jean Bernard, France*
- **Longest escalator (60 metres)** *St Petersburg underground*
- **Water pipes (1 metre)**
- **London underground (14-18 metres)**
- **Devil's hole pupfish pool (18 metres)**

GLOSSARY

BACTERIA Microscopic, single-celled organisms.

CARBONIFEROUS The 'coal-bearing' age of the Earth's history, about 345-280 million years ago.

CATACOMBS An underground cemetery.

CRUSTACEANS A group of invertebrates (animals without backbones) which includes woodlice, crabs and prawns.

CRYSTALS Regularly shaped groups of minerals.

ENVIRONMENT The particular place a plant or animal lives in and everything, living or non-living, in that place.

FOSSIL FUELS Oil, gas and coal which formed millions of years ago from the remains of prehistoric animals and plants.

GEOLOGY The scientific study of the Earth's rocks.

GEOTHERMAL ENERGY Heat energy produced naturally inside the Earth.

GERMINATION The process by which a seed develops and grows into a new plant.

GRAVITY An invisible force which pulls things down towards the centre of the Earth.

HIBERNATION A deep sleep to save an animal's energy, usually in winter.

HUMUS A jelly-like layer of rotting plant and animal matter which gives the soil its richness.

IGNEOUS Rocks formed when magma rises to the surface, cools and hardens.

LARVA (pl. larvae) The immature young of insects.

LAVA Hot, molten (liquid) rock that shoots out of volcanoes.

MAGMA Hot, molten (liquid) rock under the ground.

METAMORPHIC Igneous or sedimentary rocks which were changed by great heat and pressure inside the Earth.

MINERALS Chemicals which occur naturally inside rocks.

ORES Rocks which contain metals.

PHOTOSYNTHESIS The process by which green plants make their own food, using energy from sunlight.

SEDIMENTARY Rocks which formed in layers.

SPELEOLOGY The scientific study of caves.